Between Dreams & Reality

A Book of Poems by
Alisha Shah

VANGUARD PAPERBACK

© Copyright 2024
Alisha Shah

The right of Alisha Shah to be identified as author of this work has been asserted by her in accordance with the Copyright, Designs and Patents Act 1988.

All Rights Reserved

No reproduction, copy or transmission of this publication may be made without written permission.
No paragraph of this publication may be reproduced, copied or transmitted save with the written permission of the publisher, or in accordance with the provisions of the Copyright Act 1956 (as amended).

Any person who commits any unauthorised act in relation to this publication may be liable to criminal prosecution and civil claims for damages.

A CIP catalogue record for this title is available from the British Library.

ISBN 978-1-80016-850-3

This is a work of fiction. Names, characters, businesses, places, events and incidents are either the products of the author's imagination or used in a fictitious manner. Any resemblance to actual persons, living or dead, or actual events is purely coincidental.

Vanguard Press is an imprint of
Pegasus Elliot Mackenzie Publishers Ltd.
www.pegasuspublishers.com

First Published in 2024

Vanguard Press
Sheraton House Castle Park
Cambridge England

Printed & Bound in Great Britain

Alisha Shah

Alisha Shah is a budding young talent who has interests in a variety of fields ranging from creative writing, art, music, and sports. Alisha also volunteers at a couple of charities.

As a first-time author at only eighteen years old, Alisha started writing poetry at the age of ten. This book is a compilation of some of her exciting poems written over the past eight years, together with colourful illustrations that bring the poems to life.

Alisha has previously written two short stories and a poem that were submitted to national creative writing and poetry competitions run through schools across the UK and published by the competition organiser in a collection of short story books and a poetry book.

This previous experience provided Alisha with the confidence and impetus for writing this book.

Acknowledgements

I am grateful to my parents and my sister who have given me the encouragement, motivation and self-belief for this book project and to achieve my goals and dreams.

Thank you to each and every reader of this book.

I hope that "*Between Dreams & Reality*" inspires you to your own poetic writing journey.

As my father says: "Nothing is impossible, impossible is nothing!"

Table of Contents

FESTIVAL FEVER

Christmas Cheer	22-23
Happy Halloween!	24-25
Diwali	26-27

FANTASY

Magic Books	10-11
Magic Mirror	12-13
Magical Doors	14-15
Dark Night Creatures	16-17
The Haunted House	18-19

Meandering through Nature

Earth	30-31
Life on Earth	32-33
The Countryside	34-35
Starry Nights	36-37
Flowers	38-39
Leaves	40-41
Under the Sea	42-43

The Life as I See

Butterflies	74-75
Time	76-77
Sleep	78-79
Silence	80-81
Memory Recall	82-83
Free Me!	84-85
Courage	86-87
A Place Like Space	88-89
School Time	90-91
Maths	92-93
Painting	94-95
Musical Beats	96-97
Sports	98-99
Golf	100-101
City Life	102-103
Covid-19 Lockdown	104-105
Mobile Phone	106-107
Firefighters	108-109
Evacuee	110-111
Airplane Ride	112-113
India	114-115
Life is...	116-117
Poetry To Me	118-119

FOUR SEASONS

Spring	46-47
Rain	48-49
A Glimpse of Summer	50-51
Autumn Breeze	52-53
Snow	54-55

Animal World

Turtle Shuffle	58-59
I Once Was A Caterpillar	60-61
On Safari	62-63
Safari Animals	64-65
Life as an Ant	66-67
Snow Giant	68-69
Snow Leopard	70-71

FANTASY

Magic Books

When I open this book,
Magic jumps out,
Fiery dragons,
And fighting princesses,
Waiting for your command.

Another adventure,
In different worlds,
Meeting new people,
Seeing new places,
That nobody knows.

Glowing objects,
And powerful spells,
Miraculously transporting you,
To something or somewhere new,
That nobody knows.

With warriors,
Or Gods,
You never know,
What will happen as you marvel,
And play with your infinite vivid imagination.

MAGIC MIRROR

A beam of light shone into my eyes,
Like a sharp object glowing,
While everyone was fast asleep,
I squinted my eyes open without showing.

When I slowly woke up,
The magic mirror looked up,
As I walked over, I knocked over a cup,
Gently touching the mirror, something opened up.

My hand stretched through it,
It then pulled my legs,
I reached for my bag,
Not wanting to lag.

Where was I being transported,
In the middle of the night,
No time to waste,
Lest the adventures escape.

Magical Doors

Go and open the multi-coloured door,
There might be a magical colourful land
full of everything you have ever dreamed of.

Go and open the red door,
You might see some mystical wild animals
sniffing and circling to catch their prey.

Go and open the black door,
The door that might take you
a century back in time.

Go and open the yellow door,
You might find gold waiting for you
at the end of the rainbow.

DARK NIGHT CREATURES

Hissing snakes surrounding a glistening mound of gold,

Werewolves jumping out of their den so dark and cold,

Deadly vampires spying through hidden keyholes
in the cob webbed dungeons,

Rotting skeletons creeping around the eerie streets
leaving a pungent trail in their wake,

Bats flying around searching for their prey
with their piercing fire-coloured eyes,

Is this a dream or a nightmare through one's eyes?

Only time will tell.

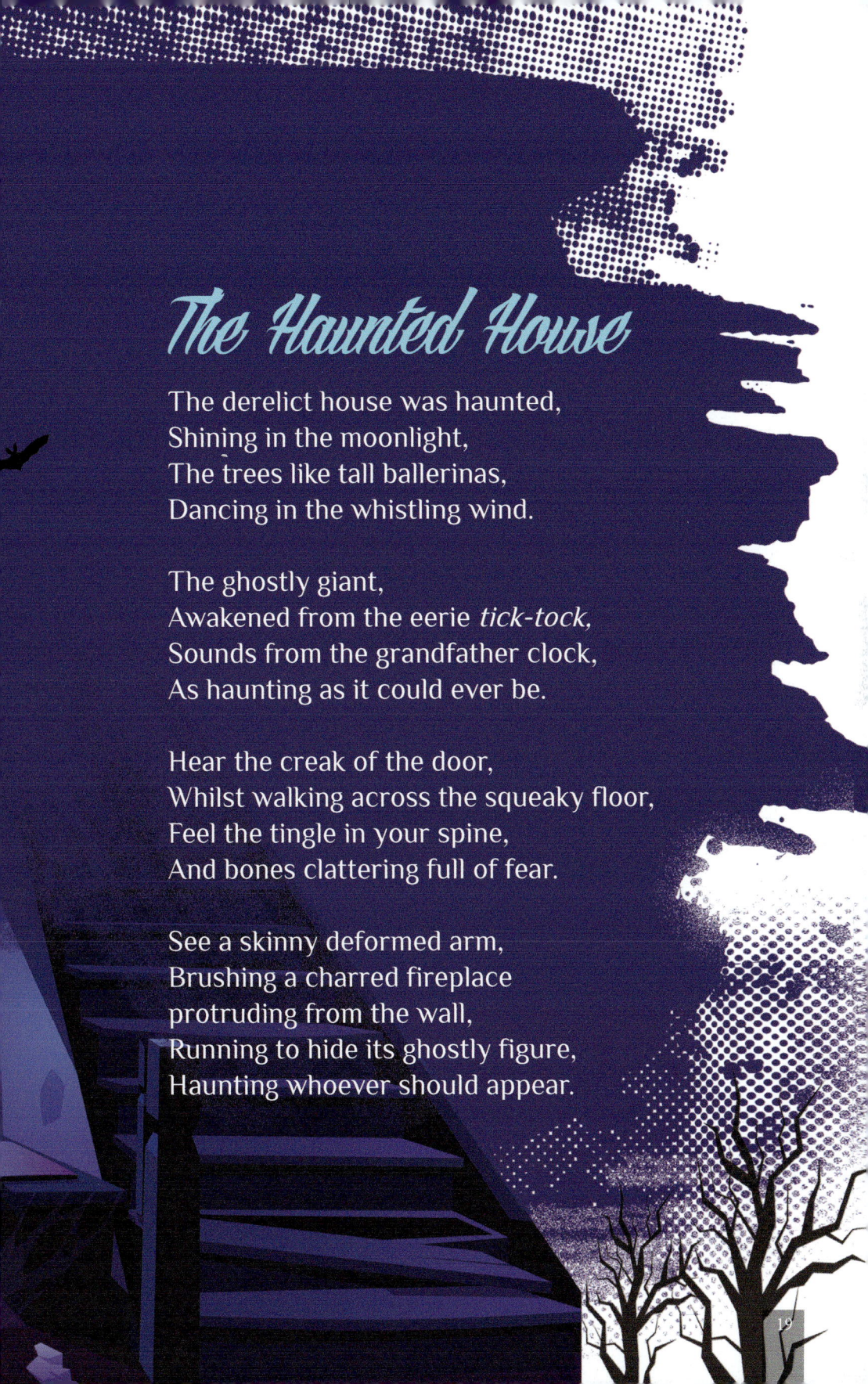

The Haunted House

The derelict house was haunted,
Shining in the moonlight,
The trees like tall ballerinas,
Dancing in the whistling wind.

The ghostly giant,
Awakened from the eerie *tick-tock,*
Sounds from the grandfather clock,
As haunting as it could ever be.

Hear the creak of the door,
Whilst walking across the squeaky floor,
Feel the tingle in your spine,
And bones clattering full of fear.

See a skinny deformed arm,
Brushing a charred fireplace
protruding from the wall,
Running to hide its ghostly figure,
Haunting whoever should appear.

Christmas Cheer

The night before Christmas brings faith,
Down the chimney filled with grace,
He hides below the cave like smoke,
Bellowing out from his throat: *Ho Ho Ho*.

Making your dream come true,
He brings hope to you,
The blessings he brings your way,
That will truly make your day.

A flick of a trick from his hat,
Brings a spell of love,
A sprinkling of a secret potion,
Fills the home full of happiness and devotion.

A family arrives,
In a loving bond,
The joyfulness of sharing,
Makes Christmas so caring.

These Christmas values,
Mean a lot for all,
Christmas is not a dream,
But a gift of love for all beings.

Happy Halloween!

Gobbling up my dinner,
Before the devils arrive,
Blood like stains start dropping,
To give them a surprise.

The first bell rings,
To have a trick or treat,
They go to the houses they dare to get in,
And soon it's my turn to trick for a sweet.

All around the neighbourhood,
Bags have a feast,
Of the frozen sugar being trapped in such haste,
To try and keep anger away from the beasts.

As the night gets darker,
The devils hide in bed,
Soon not even one decides to ring,
Until Halloween beckons again.

Diwali

The special day has come,
Each decoration box opened with joy,
Following a tradition to deck the halls,
With tinsel, rangoli, flowers and candles.

Spending extra time in the kitchen,
Making the mixtures form,
The sweets cool down,
Before the blast at dawn.

The celebrations have begun,
Colourful costumes parade in the festival of light,
As the sparks burst into colours,
Above the manicured garden lawns.

The festival of light is a kaleidoscope of colour,
Brightening up the pale blue sky,
To create marble-like patterns,
Welcoming a HAPPY NEW YEAR!

Meandering through Nature

Earth

When I look at the world map,
I wonder about its shape,
An elephant's ear or even a boot,
Just proves the wonders of the world.

Physical and human features make up the Earth,
By the wonderful buildings and beauty of nature,
That compete for attention and space,
Yet collaborate to create a meaningful place.

Hurricanes and tsunamis are natural weather patterns,
Whereas wars and environmental destruction are
of human creation,
Some of these happen without any warning,
Whilst the arms race warns of man's own
self-destruction.

Just look all around at artificial things new,
Soon in the future these will be obsolete,
Is this a human race or a rat race?
Maybe earth is all that'll be left behind in the end.

Life on Earth

When I look around me,
I see creatures of mother nature,
Going about their own business,
As time passes by.

I hear people whisper and shout,
To the others around them,
And listen to the trees whispering to each other,
Waving their hands to the beat of the breeze.

I smell the fresh air swirling around,
And the sense of creatures cooking,
Mouth-watering food in a sea of spices,
Tasting the saliva slither around my mouth.

All around me I see the wonders of nature,
Leaves, trees and animals too,
Competing for air, food and water,
In a melting pot of life on earth.

The Countryside

When I smell the freshness of the grass,
My nose tingles in the sweet smell of pollen,
The light green blanket,
Lays bare across the fields.

The tall chocolate brown branches,
Swaying their giant hands left to right,
Shaking the burgundy leaves off,
Its strong wrinkly fingers.

I hear the proud ram call the lamb,
And the young robin chirping,
As the chimes from the blowing wind,
Meanders through the majestic trees.

Starry Nights

When I see the glistening diamonds,
Giving signals to the people below,
I wonder if there might be one for me.

Trillions of stars shining brightly,
Across the navy-blue moonlit sky,
Trying to find the perfect spot to seek attention.

Only one out of all,
Stands out the most,
From its beautiful glittery dress worn to the ball.

'Tis late, we have to say goodbye,
As the gems slowly fade away,
To rest and come back on another clear moonlit night.

Flowers

A tiny seed planted in the moist soil,
Tightly snuggled in the ground,
Hoping to break free one day.

As weeks go by,
Leaves start to pop out the soil,
Reaching out to say a long hi.

Soon the time arrives,
For the little buds,
To eventually bloom.

Fully bloomed,
The emerald grass that it once was,
Turns into a landscape of coloured bombs.

Leaves

The leaves waving their hands,
As they say goodbye,
To their neighbours,
To swiftly fly up high,
In the early morning blue sky.

Brittle and crunchy Autumn leaves,
Tinted chocolate brown and fiery orange,
Daintily falling down from their trees.

As the leaves fly off,
They listen and dance,
To the tune of the whistling wind.

The sun peering through the clouds,
Watching the leaves twirl elegantly towards the sky,
And seeing the tweeting birds,
Drift away in the sapphire blue sky.

Under the Sea

The surface shimmering like gold,
Elegantly swaying in the underwater motion,
Whilst holding treasures that are new and old.

Above the gleaming surface,
A whole new world,
With creatures living life at their own pace.

Sea-life have their own underwater world,
Their coral houses,
That lie upon the sandy roads,

The water so blue,
Hiding the fantasy underneath,
That once no one knew.

Sea life is crying,
From human mistakes that must be reversed,
To save their world from dying.

FOUR
SEASONS

Spring

In spring, the moon rises later,
In spring, the sun rises earlier,
In spring, the warmth of the sun starts
burning through the cold mist.

Pink, silky, tiny,
Blossoms start to bloom on the deciduous trees,
Whilst slowly dancing down,
Making a pink carpet show beneath.

This is the time when new-born animals arrive,
Crackling and whining out of their shell,
Taking its first gasp of warm moist air to survive.

What a picture-painted landscape it is,
As the snow thaws,
The colourful shoots of nature become
the first symbol of spring.

Rain

The rain drops tap dancing on the window,
And the umbrellas start to cry,
The clouds block out the shimmering light,
Everything starts to sigh.

As the music starts to play,
Pita pata pita pata pita pata,
Diamonds dangle from the leaves,
Falling like swords cutting through
the soft ground.

The miserable day,
Makes people stay,
When the rain dribbles down each leaf,
It begins to sway.

As the day ends,
With everyone depressed,
The sun comes out,
And the sadness washes away.

A Glimpse of Summer

Sometimes a glimpse of summer arrives,
When locals roam in shorts after just a day of sun,
When your nose inhales the nostalgic scent of sunscreen,
When you finally feel a sticky drop fall from your forehead,
When your socials are filled with pool pictures,
When you can finally roam around sockless,
When you begin to realise you are allergic to pollen,
When your feet can experience the real waters,
Is when there sometimes is a glimpse of summer.

Sometimes a glimpse of summer arrives,
When nights feel as hot as days,
When umbrellas have a different use,
When the surface is filled with coloured petals,
When you start to smell the salty waters,
When sand gets in between your toes,
When ice becomes your best friend,
When all you can hear is the squidging of flip-flops,
Is when there sometimes is a glimpse of summer.

Autumn Breeze

The crunchy leaves elegantly falling off the trees,
Peeping through the impenetrable wall of mist,
I could see the sunlight beaming through the shaded trees.

As I walk across the scattered leaves,
Many glistening Conker shells appear like ghosts,
Upon the sweeping wind blowing across the shrivelled decaying matter.

I could hear the colossal oak tree,
Bellowing out a leaf storm furiously with all its might,
Shaking out all the bad energy whilst waving its hands.

The smell of damp grass tickling through my nostrils,
Triggering a volcano-like reaction being pushed out,
That form tiny crystals in the chilled air.

As I breathed in the cold icy air,
I could feel the chill with my numbed tongue,
Autumn ushering in the cloak of winter.

SNOW

A sudden drop of white dust,
Is an alert for hoods to come up,
From dry emerald green grass,
A twist in the story has occurred.

An opening of your window blinds,
Gives a bright shock to the human eye,
The fresh trees and plants of nature,
Reflects glitter from the flakes.

Children shouting across the roads,
Ducking and diving as snowballs are thrown,
Patches left from rollings of snow,
Around the snowman that slowly formed

As intense as it can get,
Slipping and sliding on the black ice,
Dirty snow slush left behind,
Still can't take away
the overall joy of snow.

Turtle Shuffle

On the moonlit night,
Infant turtles shuffling out across the wet sand,
Attempting to sprint to the deep blue sea,
Birds grappling the turtles away,
Will the turtles win the race to freedom?

Flapping as fast as they can,
Pushing the sand away,
Excited to reach the winning line,
Like champions they dive into the sea,
The turtles reach their parents' safety.

I Once Was
A Caterpillar

Stuck in a small body,
Wriggling up trees,
And wriggling down roads,
I waited long to have wings...

Wings with vibrant colours,
Wings with shape,
Wings that draw attraction,
And wings that I would one day be able to fly with.

My next stage was being trapped in a silk sack,
A cocoon which I slept in for weeks,
The long process which transformed me,
Into the beautiful butterfly I once dreamt to be.

ON SAFARI

Bumpety, bumpety, bumpety!
We reach the safari lodge,
Dusty and muddy and in a hurry,
A special secret awaits us to be revealed.

Like a treasure chest,
A safari wonderland appears,
Peering at different animals close-up,
Zebras, giraffes, elephants and hippos!

Beautiful thatched-like lodges,
Lay peacefully waiting for guests to stay,
Roses laid out on the four-poster bed,
The fan gently blowing them away.

Tables decorated for a grand buffet dinner,
Meals fit for a king and queen of the jungle,
I couldn't help but wonder,
Were we the real feast!

Safari Animals

Inside a thorny bush,
Stomps a dull, grey monster,
Flapping its tail.

Above a chocolate trunk,
Lives a wild camouflaged beast,
Lurking amongst the bushy trees.

Head in the clouds,
A tall, yellow creature stood like a skyscraper,
With eyes like a wide-angle camera,
Capturing the footage of a prey killed below.

Beneath a murky river,
Razor-sharp teeth await,
Ready to seize and crush its innocent prey,
That struggles to pass by.

Hiding behind a steep bushy hill,
Creeps a large imposing figure,
Lying in wait with red fiery eyes.

Life as an Ant

Me...
Just a tiny creature,
Which you pick up and squeeze,
With your large unique feature.

Me...
Dreaming every night,
Of the human world,
That seems a delight.

Me...
Hoping to not get squished,
Under the feet of gentle giants,
That I hope don't wish to get me mushed.

Me...
Gazing high above,
Seeing a crispy blanket,
Softly sway down from a tree like a dove.

Snow Giant

The delicate snow,
Piling on each other,
To form a white blanket,
Ready for it to crunch on each step.

The freezing wind,
Whispering loud blows,
Fighting in every way,
To push you away.

The golden pearl,
Beaming on the glittering snow,
To show off its sparkle,
During the icy blue sunny glow.

As the night falls,
The temperature drops,
The snowy-lit eyes of the furry giant,
Keeping its camouflaged watch.

Snow Leopard

Silky Snow Leopard,
As deadly yet gentle it can ever be,
Purring like a little cat waiting for praise.

It sneakily climbs up the tall icy ridge,
And leaps back down,
Cracking the ice in a click,
Claws curled sharply to grip.

It blinds your eyes,
Golden sun dancing,
Off its majestic white fleece.

Yet for all its beauty and power,
Poachers hunt mother nature's child,
For the glory of a trophy.

The Life as I See

Butterflies

When I am excited,
I feel a spark,
My eyes widen and light up,
And my hair stands up like an electric shock.

At times my tummy starts to tingle,
And butterflies start to rumble,
Like a pressure cooker in the kitchen,
Waiting to suddenly whistle.

I ask myself,
Why do both happen to me,
What feeling do I actually sense,
But the answer sits on the fence.

I wonder what it would be,
Why am I both nervous and excited,
Why is there a hurting but a hyper feeling too,
No one seems to know, do you?

TIME

As I hear the clock *tick-tock*,
I know that time is running out,
Time is both a friend and a foe,
Tick Tock Tick Tock.

When things seem tiring,
We want time to go,
When things are exciting,
We want time to slow.

We see time everywhere,
It traps us like a bubble,
Running after time, our eyes shut close,
It's nature's way to rest time.

Analogue and digital,
12-hour and 24-hour clock,
Can time be stretched?
Only time will tell.

Sleep

Entering a whole new life,
Sometimes a horror,
And sometimes a fantasy.

Unknown of what tonight's dream might be,
And how short or long it will be,
Always stays as a mystery.

Déjà vu makes you wonder,
About the potential it could have,
From being just a dream to your reality.

One minute in your sleep,
You could feel free as a bird,
The next minute you're being
chased by a herd.

Silence

It was so silent that I heard my thoughts
rustle like leaves in a paper bag.

It was so peaceful that I heard the trees
shedding their coats of bark.

It was so still that I heard a raindrop grin
before it trickled down the windowpane.

It was so tranquil that I heard the morning earth
rolling over in its sleep and doze for a few minutes more.

It was so quiet that I heard a page in this book whisper
to its neighbour "look, it's peering at us again".

Memory Recall

As my thoughts swoosh around my head,
Trying to remember a dim and distant memory,
My body becomes tense,
I feel the anger rushing through my blood,
Trying not to break out in a bead of sweat.

When I look up at the blank ceiling,
I hear the tapping of my pen on the table,
The itching on my skull,
Makes me feel frustrated,
But I know I can conquer this moment.

The tingling in my brain,
Words flying like doves,
Aha, a light bulb just flickered in my head,
Releasing my anger,
As the memory floods in.

Free me!

Blinded by a black cloth,
Sight was restrained to reach my bare eye,
Shoved into a place by a touch like a moth,
My senses were slowly saying goodbye,
Free me!

The door creaked shut with a lock,
My sight was back with a tug of my hand,
As l saw my black shadow cast on the firm floor,
A drop of the ocean broke the serene silence,
Free me!

My tall figure that cried for help,
Followed me each step l took,
Banging for freedom my mouth was instantly shut,
Free me!

My heart started to beat like a drum,
l felt my fear suddenly appear,
My body gradually started shaking,
Free me!

Taken unwillingly made me question,
Have l no rights and nothing to save me?
Banging the door was my only option,
Free me!

COURAGE

As I gripped my hands firmly on my head,
I felt my fear suddenly appear,
My body uncontrollably shaking,
And my heart rapidly racing.

Apprehensively I glanced over my shoulder,
Then taking deep breaths counting 1,2,3,
I looked down at the never-ending cliff,
Wondering if I would ever make the descent.

There was only one thought in my mind:
"Never let the fear defeat you" I said to myself,
When doing what you want to do,
Be courageous and just do it!

A Place Like Space

A place that seems so lonely,
Yet is the thought on everyone's mind,
Is there life in space?

A place consisting of circular structures,
And rocks that breathe fire,
That float in a space surrounded by no oxygen.

A place far above the sky,
Painting a picture for humans to marvel,
As the small lights smile from above.

A place where humans experiment,
To investigate life in space,
Of what we believe are aliens.

School Time

'Tis nearly nine and all are lined up,
Chatting till the bell rings,
ding-a-ling, ding-a-ling, ding-a-ling,
The teachers come with their cups,
Giving the playground a silent hush.

Each class enter the mouth of the building,
Striding towards their form rooms,
As all are seated quietly,
Another call is here.

The whole school is gathered together,
A special day or a class assembly,
A piece of cloth light as a feather,
Is laid under a candle pot.

Time speeds up and the day passes by,
A host of lessons and targets to achieve,
Some set homework and some set coursework,
But it's not all work as there's also time to play.

MATHS

Learning number techniques is a skill in life,
The levels never stop even after reaching the top,
Numbers dancing around the head,
Like gymnasts perfecting their routines.

Each maths topic learnt,
Follows you everywhere,
From geometry to probability,
It functions in every part of life.

A relationship or a rule,
A formula to follow,
Get to grips with solving these puzzles,
As you will never escape from maths.

All these years of practice,
Struggles that are overcome,
Every silly mistake made,
Comes down to the same outcome...maths!

Painting

My fiery blood rushes around my body,
Sketching images in my head,
My paint brush armed at the ready.

Like a magic wand,
The spell makes the brush dance,
Letting out the magic from within.

Each blob of paint,
Each kaleidoscope of colour,
Hitting the ever-changing canvas.

The last few strokes of the brush,
And the final detail added,
The painting bursts to life.

Musical Beats

When I hear the music beat,
Different emotions dance in my head,
Thinking what words to write,
I jot them down with a pencil lead.

Some songs are joyful and fast,
But others are sad and smooth,
It all depends on the musical beat,
And the notes that want to sound sweet.

Happy or calm,
Sad or smooth,
Both can make you feel the groove,
And when you finally hear it, you start to move.

The notes become a score,
Quieter to louder,
Louder to quieter,
Dancing across the pages to the musical beats.

SPRTS

Outside, inside, or both,
Rain, snow, or sun,
One-handed or two,
There's always something to play.

Playing in competitions,
Hearing the crowd cheer for you,
Whilst you're catching, hitting,
or throwing something,
Brings a different exhilarating feeling.

Getting better and better,
Can take you around the world,
To meet new people,
And see stunning new countries.

GOLF

Rainy, sunny or windy,
Never gives an excuse,
To play golf.

The indoor driving range,
Is a corridor of subtle bangs,
Bangs from the club to ball contact,
Hearing the sound of the musical ping,
Knowing you've hit the club's sweet spot.

Or on the outside course,
To get used to the real game,
Imagining a big crowd seeing your success.

And the satisfaction of seeing the flight of the ball,
To the delight of it softly landing,
Bouncing on the fresh trimmed grass,
Rolling into the welcoming hole.

City Life

When the clock strikes twelve,
Hearing Big Ben cry out a dozen times,
I see the city look so quiet and dark,
But inside it's so loud and bright.

When the golden sun slowly appears,
The pink candy floss slowly turns white,
As the navy-blue hue disappears,
The birds start singing alongside their orchestra.

Then the wind starts to whisper,
The humans start working,
And the cars start to glimmer,
As the birds and animals finish their shift.

Finally, the day ends,
The golden sun slowly fades,
And the navy-blue hue reappears,
As the humans wind down in their beds for the night.

COVID-19 LOCKDOWN

For the first time in a century,
Most of the world is in lockdown,
Could it just be nature's act made,
Or could it just be a political charade?

Every century on …20,
A new story occurs,
Pandemic virus spreading different from the past,
Could it get worse than the last?

Positives and negatives are always there,
To the wildlife free with no threat,
Yet for us humans not allowed out,
Would our daily lives be disturbed throughout?

No schools, no gyms, bare offices,
No personal interaction with the outside world,
With lockdown extending faster and faster,
When is corona going to get over?

MOBILE PHONE

My hands suddenly start to burn,
With bloodshot liquid,
Painfully rushing through,
As I tightly grip my cold black phone.

As I tapped a coloured icon,
Up pops an app,
In front of my eyes,
On my cold black phone.

I try to search for something,
A red-light shines catching my eye,
Something is dying,
Nooo, it's my cold black phone.

Firefighters

The firefighters spray with all their might,
Beaming light shooting through the air,
Liquid life savers fall on the fires,
To rescue the broken hearts.

The firefighters carefully search in shock,
The decimated walls of smouldering buildings,
Going through the burning smoke,
To rescue the broken hearts.

The firefighters gently dig,
Finding burnt bodies amongst rotting skeletons,
Lying beneath the wall of dust,
To rescue the broken hearts.

The firefighters save some of the trapped people,
To the cheering crowds and roar of the fire engines,
Bringing loved ones together again,
To rescue the broken hearts.

Evacuee

I opened the creaking door,
Watching my shadow cast along the floor,
My tear drops suddenly, splat!
Tip tap.

My tall figure,
Followed me all the way,
Like a spy incognito,
Tip tap.

An instant smell of a rusty engine,
Brushed by my tingling nose,
A long piece of metal tapping along a track,
Tip Tap.

Crying my eyes out,
I wave goodbye,
To my beloved family,
Tip tap.

AIRPLANE RIDE

I had just settled into my airplane seat,
And my seat began to vibrate,
I felt all the bumps of the concrete floor,
As the airplane slowly moved across the runway.

The long wait in the airport had sped by,
As the large metal dragon prepared itself for flight,
Its wings spread out and angled for take-off,
Launched into the air like a ball from a catapult.

No sooner had we taken off,
It was already time for landing,
The dragon circling above finding a space to rest,
Amongst the ant-like houses and cars,
Glistening in the blinding sun below.

The dragon settles down without a hitch,
Its wings hot from the journey,
Now it's time for it to rest,
And reset for its next flight of adventure.

A sudden arrival of a blast of scents,
The smell of freshly cooked spices,
And the joyful lives at the colourful events.

Every corner a different tradition,
A range of favourite foods,
And shining festivals across the nation.

A place like India full of culture and beauty,
From forts to castles and temples too,
These wonders really fulfil their duty.

A truly amazing country this is,
A huge part of Asia itself,
And a country not to be missed.

India is a place of peace and transformation,
Where animals are treated holy,
And where culture is the definition of this great nation.

Life is...

Life is facing the fantasy we all wish we had,

Life is overcoming the struggles we never wished we came across,

Life is coming across people that positively change your perspective,

Life is meeting people for better, for worse, for richer, for poorer, to love one another,

Life is setting and working towards your goals,

Life is living the dream you aimed to achieve,

Life is a continuous journey of learning for the better,

Life is making mistakes you learn and grow from,

Life is making the most of your current life and be the best that you can be.

Poetry to Me

I enjoy the literacy of poetry,
But sometimes it can be a mystery,
My imagination electrified by
the possibilities,
With ideas that pop-up
as collaboration.

To show my joy for poetry,
I wrote this book to share its
love and empathy,
Towards the ideas that
dance around my head,
When soundly sleeping through
the night.

Illustrated & Designed by:

honeycomb
creative support(p)limited

www.honeycombindia.net